# "Painting My Life"

## "How Vitiligo Impacted My History."

### Karina Cuestas

! God Love Us!

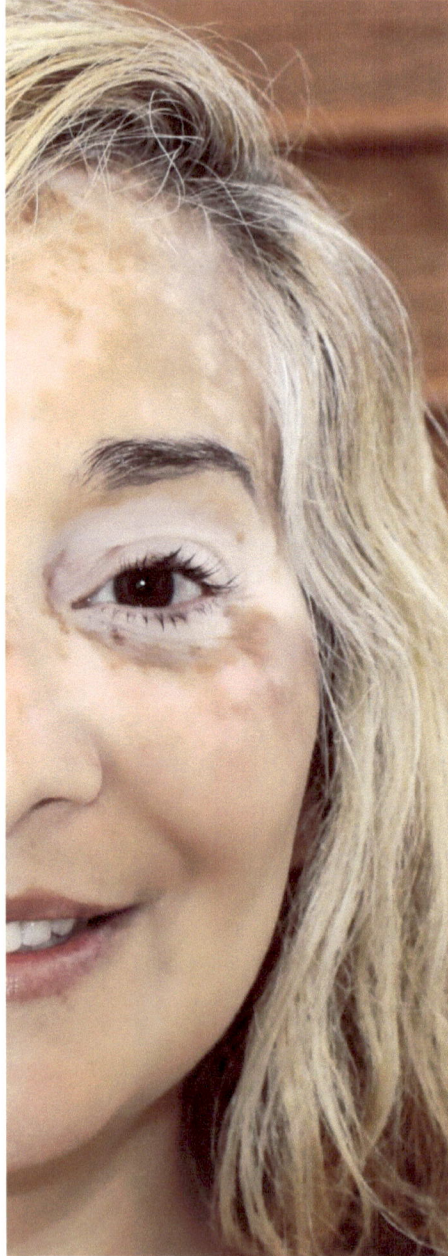

Karina Cuestas-2024

# "To My Inner Child."

I dedicate this book to my inner child. I want her to know that I love her deeply and thank her for being such a strong, kind-hearted, and charming little girl. I am grateful to her for finding me again after so many years. It's beautiful to know that she is in my heart, and I promise to care for her, love her, respect her, and value her. "You are a beautiful daughter of God, unique and irreplaceable in this world."

*" The strength to move forward is found when we accept that every obstacle is an opportunity to rediscover ourselves and move forward with more determination, when the path seems uncertain."*

# Table of Contents

- "To my Inner Child." ……………………….... 6
- Introduction……………………………….......... I3

Chapter 1: "How My Story Begins." ……........... 15

- The First Years
- The Beginning of Vitiligo
- Initial Treatment an Emotional Roller Coaster."
- A New Treatment and Frustrated Hope
- Reflections of Karma

- Chapter 2: Shadows of the Mirror……………... 25

- The Beginning of Teasing
- The Fight for Acceptance
- The Disenchanted
- Strength Through Creativity
- The Love of Learning
- A World Without Internet

- **Chapter 3: "Through Sunburn: A Challenging Experience"** .......................................... 33

    - Sun Exposure
    - "Consequences of Sun Exposure Without Sunscreen."
    - Lessons Learned

- **Chapter 4: "Facing Challenges and Finding Empowerment."** ........................….......... 39

    - "High School: The Beginning of a A New Stage."
    - A Broken Heart
    - "My Last Two Years of High School At a Private School."
    - "The Private School Became My Refuge."

- **Chapter 5: Reflections on Educational Differences**............................................. 47

  - Reflection on Public Schools vs Private Schools
  - Teaching Respect
  - Good Education Goes Through a Good Example
  - The Importance of a Good Teacher
  - Choose Good Friends

- **Chapter 6: "Authentic Colors in a Monochromatic World."** ................... 53

  - The pressure for the Use of Makeup
  - Being Authentic but Not Invisible

- **Chapter 7: "Discovering My Value."** ............ 57

  - Toxic Relationships
  - "How Childhood Experiences Led Me to Choose the Wrong Partners.'
  - "Embracing My Authenticity and Self-Steam."

- Hitting Rock Bottom
- Looking to the Future with Hope

- **Chapter 8: "A New Chapter of My Life."** ....... 65

  - Focusing on my Goals
  - Encounter with God

- **Chapter 9: "Strength Through Adversity."** ..... 75

  - "My Mother: An Example of Life."
  - Facing Challenges

- **Chapter 10: "Reflections of Strength: Embracing My Authenticity."** .......................... 81

  - Self Love
  - New Era

- **Biography**................................................ 87

# Introduction

In childhood, shapes and colors were our way of discovering the world. Still, that discovery came with a notable difference: vitiligo. From the tender age of four, I noticed changes in my skin color, and over time, I came to understand the emotional toll of living with this skin condition. The deep pain caused by being mocked by others made me feel lonely and unloved, but it also helped me discover my inner strength. This book will be an intimate account of my journey with vitiligo, a journey of self-discovery that includes difficulties, challenges, and the profound experience of self-love.

# Chapter One

## "How My Story Began."

The summer of 1983 marked a change in my life. At the age of four, an unexpected diagnosis came as a surprise, "vitiligo," a skin color condition unknown at that time to many, entered my childhood world, unleashing a series of events that would change my life forever.

In this chapter, we will see the discovery of this disease and the unwavering courage of my parents. Despite the devastating news, they showered me with love and support, tirelessly searching for a solution for this skin condition. Their strength in the face of adversity is truly inspiring.

# The Beginning of Vitiligo

Like any girl, I spent my first four years playing and getting into mischief. I remember being a happy girl, and I was not aware of how cruel some people could be just for being different. At that stage of my life, there were no differences in color or race; there was only love for oneself and others.

Vitiligo began to manifest itself in me when I was four years old. My mom noticed a tiny white spot on my face and a white eyelash. When my parents saw this, they were distressed and did not know what it could be. They quickly took me to the dermatologist, who explained that I suffered from a disease called vitiligo. The dermatologist explained to my parents that vitiligo is an incurable disease that causes skin depigmentation. When the immune system attacks the melanocytes, white spots appear on various body areas, eventually resulting in a complete loss of skin color. In addition, vitiligo also affects hair color since in areas where the skin lacks pigmentation, the hair also turns white. Vitiligo can be caused by autoimmune and environmental factors.

## '' Initial Treatment and ''Emotional Roller Coaster.'

The dermatologist prescribed me some medicine to take for an indefinite period and a cream that I had to apply to my face daily and exposed myself to the sun for a few minutes every morning. Furthermore, he warned my parents that in the future, when I entered adolescence, I would need to use makeup to cover the white spots on my face because people who suffer from that condition can experience psychological damage and affect their self-esteem because of it.

The effects that the medicine caused me when taking it were stomach pain, nausea, and vomiting. I still remember the taste of the pill and how sick it made me when I was taking it. Despite the harmful effects of the medication, I continued to take it under the belief of my parents that it could cure my vitiligo.

However, the pills did not produce the desired results and accelerated the spread of the white spots on my skin. In just three months, I was with half of my face white, white spots appeared around my eyes, eyebrows, forehead, skull, side of my cheeks, chest, back, and feet. Also, my hair started to turn white, and my eyelashes became white. Sometimes, my skin color reappeared on my face, and then it disappeared. As the white spots began to appear on my face, my parents were not just dealing with physical changes but also emotional ones. They had to face uncomfortable looks and questions from people.

My parents also suffered a lot from the pain they felt when they saw me with vitiligo on my face and the frustration of not seeing their daughter cured of that condition. I remember I was more distressed by seeing the reaction of my family and other people towards me than by having white spots on my face. I was a child, and I still did not fully understand what was happening to me. Yet, their emotional journey was as significant as mine, if not more, and our unity and support for each other helped us through this challenging time.

As the years passed, no positive improvements were seen in my skin condition, and my health condition worsened due to the negative influence of the medicine. The disappointment and frustration of failed treatments took a toll on my emotional well-being, as well as my physical health. I am not saying the medicine the dermatologist recommended is not good for others. I am only talking about my personal experience, which did not help me; on the contrary, they accelerated the spread of white spots.

Consequently, my father made the difficult decision to end this treatment. According to my mother, in an act of frustration and pain, when my father saw me suffering, he threw the pills into the toilet.

## *A New Treatment and a Frustrated Hope*

My parents kept looking for what other medicine they could get that would help me heal. They learned of a man selling some natural oils to drink that cured vitiligo. This man claimed that the medicine consisted of oils made from herbs, although the herbs' specifications were unknown. My family took the leap of faith to buy the medication, hoping it could cure me. Despite our financial situation, which was not so good, my parents showed incredible dedication. Despite its excessive cost, they worked tirelessly to gather the necessary resources to get the treatment.

This treatment lasted a year, and the procedure consisted of taking a bottle of oil daily on an empty stomach. When I started taking the herbal oils, I noticed that, in certain instances, my skin recovered some pigmentation.

This improvement was for a brief time since the white spots appeared later. After taking these oils for a year, I saw no improvement either. The repeated disappointments from these failed treatments took a toll on my hope.

Throughout this process, my parents learned of the existence of doctors in Cuba who had effective medication for vitiligo. However, due to our financial limitations, they could not afford to travel to Cuba and undergo such treatment. After my parents saw that none of the medicines they tried cured me, they were forced to accept the possibility that I could live with vitiligo for the rest of my life.

## Reflections on Karma

Also, my mother shares with me the perspective that what happened could have been a kind of karma. When my father was younger, he used to make fun of a young woman affected by vitiligo. This young woman endured their laughter and cruel nicknames every time they crossed paths.

According to my mother, when I started having Vitiligo, my father's regret for the pain he inflicted on that young woman became palpable as he saw my face affected by the same condition. Even though I share a tremendous physical similarity with my father, I cannot help but question whether what I experienced resulted from karma. I may have had to face the consequences of my father's earlier mistakes so that he could learn a lesson.

This experience provided him with the opportunity to confront his guilt and remorse as he saw his daughter dealing with vitiligo. His transformation from someone who once caused pain to someone who now empathizes, and supports is genuinely inspiring.

Despite my condition, I was always a girl of undeniable internal and external beauty. Whether or not it is karma, I do not consider this question relevant since I understand that perfection is unattainable. We all make mistakes in our lives. I have come to accept and embrace my condition, and I know that this deeply affected my parents as they watched me face this autoimmune disease. I appreciate their persistent efforts to seek a cure for me.

Karina Cuestas- 1983 before vitiligo

Karina Cuestas- 1983- After Vitiligo

*"When we don't understand what happens to us, we must remember that God always has a greater purpose for our lives, even amid uncertainty."*

# Chapter Two

## "Shadows of the Mirror."

I noticed my classmates' rejection from the beginning of my school life. Their laughter and hurtful comments took over and made me feel worthless. They led me to question my worth and my place at school. In this chapter, I share the emotional difficulties I went through and how I tried to find the strength to move forward.

# The Beginning of Teasing

A year later, when I started elementary school, I entered the Cacique Calarcá School in Ibagué, Tolima, Colombia. I remember with excitement the beginning of this new phase in my life, in which I longed to learn and show friendships. Unfortunately, from the start, I began to perceive the ridicule and rejection of my classmates by calling me whatever nicknames they could think of. Laughter and hurtful comments became a constant presence, making me feel less valuable. Like I did not belong at that school.

# The Fight for Acceptance

The cruelty of some students baffled me, as I longed to be part of his circle of friends. My childish mind did not understand the reason for his hostility, which plunged me into profound sadness as I felt excluded. However, I would soon become aware that my entry into the school world would be marked by a reality that would distinguish me: "vitiligo." As time passed and life at school became every day, I found myself increasingly exposed to looks, words and gestures of displeasure.

The children made fun of me, associating vitiligo with a contagious disease called ringworm, which also causes white spots on the face. These misperceptions distanced me from some classmates, who were afraid to approach me. They called me insults like "contagious" and made fun of my appearance, giving me nicknames like "Coffee with Milk" and "Dairy Cow."

Ignorance about vitiligo made me feel helpless. I did not understand why children made fun of me. My classmates' incomprehension affected the way I saw myself. When I got home, I looked in the mirror and saw a beautiful girl, but I cried because I did not understand why the other children treated me like that. The depigmented and two-colored skin spoke for me. I felt very confused and vulnerable in a world that was not familiar with vitiligo. I did not understand that being different from others was okay and that I did not have to be the same as others to be accepted. Despite all the teasing towards me, I always tried to make friends and did my best not to let it affect me emotionally. I was always affectionate with my classmates. I never held a grudge against them, and I always forgave them.

# The Disenchanted

Most of my elementary school experiences were with my best friend then. She was a person I completely trusted and had known since first grade. We share laughter, secrets, and unforgettable moments. However, in moments of discord and arguments, everything changed. It was a profound betrayal to discover that the person I had always relied on for defense and support had become the one who could hurt me the most with her words. There were times when our opinions clashed, and arguments arose. It was natural for two friends to have differences. Still, I never imagined that those differences manifested in such a hurtful way. When she was mad at me, she said words that she knew would hurt me. My friend called me "Coffee with Milk," as if my features were a reason for ridicule and shame.

Then, I knew my physical appearance had become a vulnerability in her hands. My friend knew about my struggle with vitiligo; she was with me all the time, and she was my witness to how children made fun of me for my skin color condition. Whenever I heard the words "Coffee with Milk," I felt a direct blow to my self-esteem. It was as if the person who knew me better than anyone had used my appearance to hurt me. I felt a deep sadness and disappointment, as if the bond of trust that united us had been shattered. These words, seemingly harmless to others, carried a weight I struggled to bear. Despite the hurt, I never harbored any resentment toward her. Instead, I chose to forgive and continue our friendship. This experience and routine rejection from other children became a part of my daily life. Thanks to the unwavering support of my family and friends, I learned to be strong and move forward. Their understanding and encouragement have been instrumental in my journey.

## *Strength Through Creativity*

Despite the ridicule of my peers, I persevered and focused on my passion for artistic expression. From an early age, I channeled my feelings through songs and stories I composed, finding profound joy and fulfillment in my creativity. I remember a writing contest organized by my school. When I heard about the opportunity, I decided to write a children's book, which ultimately won first prize. This was the first book I had ever written, and it became a wonderful opportunity that set me on my path as a writer.

It wasn't long before, in my city, a poetry contest was organized, and I had the privilege of standing for my school. With God's grace, I won, which opened doors for me to gain recognition in my community. This victory led to opportunities to appear on the radio and perform in various theaters across the city, where I brought poetry to life through performance. It was a beautiful experience, one I dedicated myself to wholeheartedly for several years, blending my love for poetry with the art of theatrical expression.

In addition, I felt an even stronger desire to create. I decided to design personalized cards for special occasions such as Valentine's Day to share my creativity in a unite way. Despite my early age, I was already starting a business to earn money. I offered my colleagues my meticulously drawn and painted card creations for San Valentine's Day, accompanied by original poems that I wrote with dedication. Thus, I explored another side of my creativity. Creating and focusing my mind on something productive filled me with joy.

# The Love of Learning

My commitment to excellence was also reflected in my academic performance. Vivid memories appear, like when I was sick but still wanted to attend school because of my deep love for learning.

I remember crying and telling my mother to let me go to school, even though I had an exceedingly high fever. Such was my fervent enthusiasm for learning and constant improvement that I longed to study even with a fever. Unwavering dedication to research and the search for outstanding results have always existed. In my reflections, the image of my longing for knowledge and desire to improve in all aspects of my life persists from an early age. Although unconsciously, the coexistence of vitiligo in my life played a role in my drive to improve myself daily. Despite knowing that I would face ridicule from my classmates every time I went to school. I remember always having an unwavering dedication to studying and seeking outstanding results.

# A World Without Internet

Looking back, I appreciate that we did not have the technology and internet that are so essential in this era. Children and young people take part in more enriching activities for intellectual growth than playing video games, and the constant presence of the internet is available today because it is addictive.

The absence of these online influences contributed to creating a healthier environment conducive to children's development. This environment allowed children to explore activities that fostered learning, creativity, and meaningful social interactions, promoting a deeper connection with the world around them.

I am grateful that I did not have access to technology in my youth. This lack of technology has encouraged me to focus more on my studies and explore my creativity instead of scrolling through social media or playing video games. It was fundamental for my development in an environment where I did not fit in and needed to be better received.

# Chapter Three

## "Through Sunburn: A Challenging Experience."

In this chapter, I will discuss the painful burns I suffered due to unprotected sun exposure. I will also explore how these experiences have further deepened my impact on various aspects of my life.

### Sun Exposure

Living with vitiligo presents me with a unique set of challenges. It's not just about dealing with teasing and uncomfortable questions from others; it's also about being constantly mindful of sun exposure.

33

My skin's lack of melanin, the natural shield against ultraviolet rays, makes me more prone to sunburn. The protective role of melanin in skin color is significant; if you have pigmentation, you are at a lower risk of burns compared to vitiligo-affected skin, which lacks this crucial protection.

## *"Consequences of sun exposure without sunscreen."*

My parents often took me to the beach during my childhood. However, they didn't always take the necessary precautions to protect my skin. I spent long hours on the beach without sunscreen, leaving the depigmented areas of my skin vulnerable to the sun's harmful effects. This experience was a valuable lesson that taught me the importance of protecting our skin from solar rays. This neglect led to severe second-degree burns on the depigmented areas of my skin, causing immediate medical attention due to extensive blistering.

Going back in time, I remember the Doctor who used a needle to break the blisters precisely and then applied a special burn cream to my face. The recovery process was long and painful. As a young child, I struggled to understand the gravity of my situation, leaving a profound emotional scar on my being.

The last episode of severe sunburn occurred later, during a trip to the pool with other schoolmates. Unfortunately, I did not have sunscreen that day, so I was exposed to the sun all day. When I returned home, my skin was red and burned, and I was in a lot of pain. The night was unbearable. The burning deprived me of a restful sleep, and the visits to the mirror to see how the condition of the burn was continuing were disturbing. The inflamed appearance of my face filled me with fear. I remembered the sunburn I had had before and everything I suffered for not protecting myself from the sun's rays. The fear and regret were overwhelming.

When I faced the mirror the following day, I was shocked by my appearance's transformation. An image that I remembered from the movie "Beauty and the Beast" came to mind, with the difference that, in this case, I saw the "Beast" in the mirror. My face was so swollen that even my eyes were hidden. I suffered a lot when I saw my face so swollen, and my parents cried with anguish and pain when they saw me like that with my face burned.

My parents took measures to hide me from my sisters by placing a blanket over my face so that my sisters couldn't see my face swelling. I was quickly taken to the hospital, where the Doctor diagnosed second-degree burns on my face caused by sun exposure. The physical pain was only part of the struggle.

The emotional toll was significant, and the treatment prescribed by the Doctor was not a quick fix. It required constant effort over a long time to achieve a comprehensive recovery, both physically and emotionally. I didn't go out or go to school because I didn't want people to see me like that, with my face burned.

I remember the only times I went outside for a long time were when I had medical appointments at the hospital. Every time I went to Doctor's appointments, my parents would put a blanket over my head so that people wouldn't see my face and ask intrusive questions. These experiences left an indelible mark on my life. They instilled deep-seated fear and anxiety about unnecessary sun exposure, reinforcing my unwavering commitment to avoid the sun without adequate protection.

## *Lessons Learned*

After a long recovery, my skin finally healed from the burns, and I could return to school activities. These experiences related to sun exposure taught both my parents and me a crucial lesson: it is essential to protect the skin from the harmful effects of the sun's rays, especially considering my vitiligo condition.

Since then, I have adopted a vigilant approach to protecting my skin from the sun, using sunscreen, wearing a hat, and striving to minimize my prolonged exposure. These experiences have engraved many emotions in my soul. Through tears and pain, I have embraced a valuable lesson about the importance of protecting my skin and accepting that my skin is delicate because it does not have pigmentation and that I must take care of it. Despite the hardships, I am committed to learning from these experiences. I move forward with hope, knowing that these life lessons will continue to guide me.

*"Despite adversity, every day is an opportunity to focus on being better because personal growth is born from the challenges overcome."*

# *Chapter*
# *Four*

## *"Facing Challenges and Finding Empowerment."*

The beginning of secondary education marked a chapter of expectations and challenges as I faced ridicule from my classmates for vitiligo. However, my parents' brave decision to enroll me in a private school completely changed my school experience, giving me respect and sincere friendships. This journey is a testament to the strength we can find within ourselves.

## "High School" the Beginning of a New Stage."

After completing primary and middle school, I entered high school with the conviction that it would bring significant opportunities and transformations. Despite the challenges I knew I would face due to my vitiligo condition; I found myself figured out to overcome the obstacles and hope to achieve a more positive environment.

I thought my experience with vitiligo would take a more positive turn. Still, I soon realized that the path would be more challenging than I had imagined. The students continued to make fun of me and see me as if I were less than them because of my skin color. His mockery and comments with other classmates made my life impossible every day. My mother, seeing me sad every day when I came back from school, was determined to change schools constantly. Her care and determination were clear, but the insensitivity of some classmates was a cruel reality that persisted. Despite this, I held onto hope, believing that each new institution I arrived at might be different, might not house individuals with mean attitudes and cruelty in their words and actions.

## A Broken Heart

One particularly striking memory lingers in my mind. It happened after leaving school when I boarded the bus heading home. While seeing the landscape through the window, two young men my age came on board. Their faces expressed amazement and disgust when they saw me, as if they had seen a monster.

I remember one of them saying to the other: "With women like her, I lose the desire to be a man." Those words caused such deep pain in my heart and my self-esteem that it made me feel I was not worthy to be loved and accepted for who I am. His words left me bewildered, and I questioned my beauty. I couldn't understand why this young man reacted so negatively to my appearance when I had always felt beautiful. Vitiligo was a part of me, but this experience at the tender age of twelve left an indelible mark on my life. It was a moment of confusion but became a turning point in my journey toward self-acceptance. Those cruel words that the boy said to me were embedded very deeply in my heart, and I made a conscious decision to keep this bitter experience to myself. It was a testament to my resilience, a strength I didn't know I had.

The bullying greatly impacted my self-esteem, making me believe I would not be attractive or valuable enough to find reciprocal love. Reminding myself I was worthy and beautiful despite what others said was a constant battle. This experience made me realize the profound impact words can have. Our words can either bless someone or cause harm, potentially affecting them for the rest of their lives. Therefore, we must be mindful of what we say to others.

Another experience I had was when my mother took me to a new school to enroll. We walked up the stairs when three young students sat and started laughing at me when they saw me, not caring that my mother was present. They were so happy making fun of me, laughing aloud, and comparing me to a clown. The laughter and mockery continued, but I refused to let it break me.

Despite the pain, I kept my composure, refusing to give them the satisfaction of seeing me sad. Inside, I was hurting, but I held my head high, ignored the hurtful laughter, and continued my path without saying a word. The emotional toll was heavy, but I was determined not to let it show. Despite the continued cruelty from my classmates, I found solace in my mother's unwavering support. Even as she felt the pain of seeing me endure these situations, I stayed resolute in my decision not to show any sign of weakness or sadness to those who looked to hurt me. I was determined not to let them see me defeated. Through this ordeal, my mother also learned about the bitter reality of human insensitivity and the cruelty that some people can show for no reason.

## *"My last Two Years of High School at a Private School."*

In my last two years of high school, my mom made a brave decision that would change my life. She invested in my education and enrolled me at José de Acevedo y Gómez school in Ibagué, Tolima, Colombia. This choice was based on the hope that this school, being a private school, would provide the respectful environment I was looking for and be more welcoming to me.

I entered school with enthusiasm, although without many expectations. This decision was one of the best my mom could have made, because the students received me with the respect and appreciation that I deserved. For the first time in the school environment, I felt accepted.

My time at "José de Acevedo y Gómez" marked a radical change in my school experience. I formed sincere friendships and experienced a school environment where I was valued and respected. If they wanted to know what I had, they approached me with profound respect and without making fun of me. This transformative experience profoundly enriched my life and my personal development. It taught me the value of education and respect and showed me that children still embody these qualities.

## *"The Private School Became My Refuge."*

My journey through high school education was a testament to the fact that despite the bullying and hardship, I found refuge in a school where I finally met students who respected me despite my differences. This experience taught me the importance of the power of support in overcoming bullying.

During that period, I formed a group of friends who supported each other, always keeping treatment based on respect and affection. The enduring impact of these supportive friendships is a testament to the importance of such relationships in our lives. To this day, I keep contact with one of my friends from that school. After graduation, we each took different paths, and, unfortunately, we lost communication.

However, recently, with an ardent desire to reunite with her, I returned to Ibagué in Tolima, Colombia. After searching for her for several years, fortunately, I found where she lives, and I was able to have a beautiful encounter with her. This reunion revitalized our friendship since I never forgot that she was always with me in the last two years of my school years and always proved to be a trustworthy friend. This transformative experience taught me that kindness and politeness still prevail. Thanks to the support of my parents and their choice to invest in my education, I found a school where I felt accepted and respected. The last two years of high school were extraordinary for me. This story reminds me that we can forge our path to a brighter future even amid adversity.

Karina Cuestas-1993

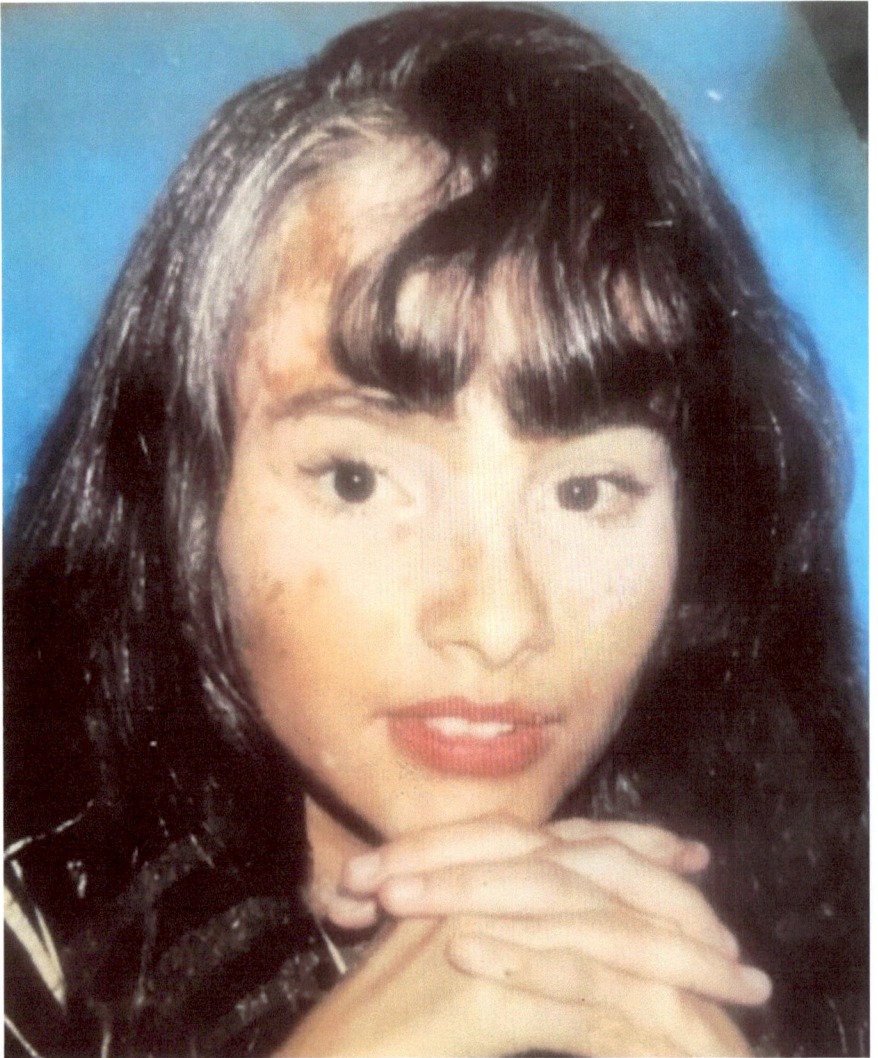

# Chapter Five

## Reflections on Educational Differences

This chapter discusses the importance of educating children from an early age. Additionally, we will examine whether there are differences between public and private schools, considering how these educational environments influence the development of interpersonal relationships and social values.

# Reflection on Public Schools vs. Private Schools

I reflected on the stark differences between my schooling experiences at public and private institutions. This reflection underscores the need for a more inclusive education system. My last two years of school were transformative. The private school became a sanctuary where I found peace and acceptance. This positive experience in a private school is a beacon of hope for a more inclusive and respectful education system. For the first time, after 10 years of ridicule, I found myself in a school that not only respected me but also considered my feelings, something I had long craved. This experience raised an intriguing question: What differentiates private and public schools?

I do not want to imply that, at that time, public schools lacked respectful students with values. I spent ten years in a public school, and I always kept good values, as did many of my classmates. Today, we have excellent public institutions and students who stand out for their respect and good behavior. However, my personal experience did not reflect the respectful environment in which most of the students in my city's public schools were during that time.

## Teaching Respect

This explains the importance of teaching children respect for others early on. Education is a complex process that goes beyond getting academic knowledge. It involves the comprehensive training of individuals capable of understanding others, respecting differences, and functioning in society. In this context, parenting and guidance are essential in laying the foundation of values and principles that will guide children throughout their lives, including their school experience. If all parents made this commitment, they could significantly improve the school experience of children who face challenges like those I experienced in the past.

## Good Education Goes Through a Good Example

Children are sponges that absorb information from their environment; they see how their parents relate to others and face challenging situations. When parents give a strong example of mutual respect and acceptance, children develop a deeper understanding of the importance of treating everyone with consideration and empathy. Parenting and guidance impact family life and the school community. Children who grow up with good values tend to be more respectful, understanding, and willing to collaborate with their peers. This creates a more positive school environment of respect and consideration for other students.

## The Importance of a Good Teacher

I also understand the fundamental importance that teachers have in teaching mutual respect. They can promote positive values among students by setting up clear rules and expectations about how students should behave in the classroom and with their peers outside of it. Teachers also play an essential role in teaching how to resolve conflicts respectfully and take immediate action if they detect disrespectful behavior towards themselves or others. Moreover, teachers must involve parents in reinforcing these values. Parents are essential in their children's education, and their involvement is critical to creating an environment of respect for others in school classrooms.

## Choose Good Friends

Friendships also play an essential role in the children's behavior. As the saying goes, "Tell me who you hang out with, and I'll tell you who you are." spending time with a person over an extended period tends to influence and shape us in a certain way. Education from an early age is critical; the educator and guidance and support are necessary for creating an environment that teaches and celebrates the value of respect for others and the ability to make good behavioral decisions, regardless of the influences of other friends.

It all starts at home. When parents lead by example, teaching their children to respect others, and when teachers instill strong values in their students, and students choose friends with good values and principles, we lay the foundations for a respectful society.

*"Good education begins at home, but it is strengthened by the example of a good teacher and enriched by the positive influence of friendships."*

# Chapter Six

## "Authentic Colors in a Monochromatic World."

In this chapter, I will share my teenage struggle with accepting myself, especially with facial vitiligo, in a world that constantly pressured me to hide it. You'll understand how I embraced my authenticity over conforming to societal norms. My journey to self-acceptance became a source of strength, proving that authenticity is more valuable than conforming to superficial standards. My story inspires you to embrace your true self.

## The Pressure for the Use of Makeup

As I went through the complex challenges of adolescence, I faced a dilemma that challenged me at every turn: how to respond to my family's well-intentioned suggestions and advice that rained down on me to hide the vitiligo on my face. Many people treated skin spots, unique and beautiful in their way, as blank canvases that needed to be corrected. The pressure to camouflage my appearance and submit to the world's aesthetic homogeneity often became overwhelming.

## Being Authentic but Not Invisible

Amidst the conflicting opinions, like I need to cover my face with a heavy foundation, I consciously decided in my teenage years to embrace my authenticity. I chose to dye my hair, which was already turning white, and not hide my differences under layers of makeup like some people did. This choice was empowering and impactful. My beauty routine was limited to the essentials: mascara to enhance my eyes and a touch of pink lipstick for my lips, constantly reminding me of the confidence I radiated from within. As an adult, I also allowed a hydrating tint to join my routine because it gives my skin a healthy glow without hiding the spots that make me unique. It was a carefully balanced decision, a reminder that being authentic didn't mean being invisible. Choosing not to give in to the temptation of a heavy foundation was a crucial decision. It symbolized my determination not to hide the vitiligo. I knew that if I started hiding behind layers of makeup, I would betray my appearance and essence. Every spot on my skin was a testament to my experiences and personal stories, and I chose to wear those stories with pride.

The confidence from facing the world as I am, without fear of criticism or judgment, made me realize that my authenticity was more valuable than the ideas of other superficial people who seek perfection. This conscious decision to embrace my identity led me to discover a solid, proud confidence I had never experienced. It's a reminder that our authenticity is our most asset, far more precious than the fleeting standards of perfection set by others. Every day became an opportunity to challenge norms and celebrate authenticity in all its forms, constantly remembering that it was worth being true to myself in a world that often tried to mold us in it.

Karina Cuestas-1992

# Chapter Seven

## "Discovering My Value."

In this chapter, I will dive into the toxic relationships and the impact of the bullying I received in my childhood and adolescence. These experiences influenced my decisions in adulthood and led me to a relationship with the wrong man. However, I found myself through the lessons I learned. These lessons included setting boundaries, recognizing red flags, and prioritizing myself.

## Toxic Relationships

My journey through love has been challenging and marked by toxic relationships. I was with men who betrayed, manipulated me, and broke my trust. Men who made me feel inferior and lucky to be with them, weakening my self-esteem. Despite the negativity and abuse, I found the strength to leave these unhealthy relationships for my own good. This journey taught me to understand my choices in love and rebuild my self-esteem.

## "How Childhood Experiences Led Me to Choose the Wrong Partners.'

Over time, I discovered this reality by reflecting on my childhood experiences. I understood that my personal history, how I grew up, and the experiences that affected my life growing up played an essential role in choosing my romantic relationships as an adult. Unfortunately, as an adult, I not only faced relationships in which I was deceived, manipulated, mocked, and used, but I also relived my childhood feelings of being teased for having vitiligo.

## The Cruelty of Some Men

One of those painful moments was when an ex-boyfriend used vitiligo as an emotional weapon. When I confronted him and expressed my desire to end the relationship with him because of the psychological abuse he was subjecting me to, he made fun of my appearance. He made hurtful comments about me, telling me what he thought I was with those white spots on my face.

What he wanted to tell me was that I was less than him because I had vitiligo and, therefore, I didn't have the right to end the relationship. This cruel response left me disappointed and bewildered, wondering how an adult could use my skin condition to hurt, manipulate me, and make me feel like I was less than him. Despite everything, I kept a firm stance, making it clear to him that I would not get back with him, that his words did not affect my self-esteem, and that I am worth a lot as a woman, regardless of my vitiligo.

Another relationship I had was marked by teasing about my appearance, this time during my pregnancy. Even though I was expecting my daughter, my daughter's father belittled my image with hurtful comments about having vitiligo on my face. I know that he did it to lower my self-esteem so that he could feel more than me. Despite the disappointments in that relationship, my greatest gift was my daughter, whom I raised as a single mother. My path was full of challenges, but every struggle and sacrifice contributed to raising my daughter, obtaining a college education, and continuing to work with my art.

## *"Embracing My Authenticity and Self-Esteem."*

Despite my adulthood, I am continuously facing negative comments related to my condition, especially from older people who question my appearance. Recently, at my workplace, a man asked me a direct question about my face, asking me what had happened to me. I explained to him that I have vitiligo, to which he responded with pity, expressed compassion, and suggested that I should feel ashamed about the way I look. This situation perplexed me, as I could not believe what I heard. I responded to the man by saying, "Why should I feel bad? I am alive and in good health. Also, my whole family is fine. I'm happy"."

Also, while heading to my Zumba class at the gym, a woman was curious about the white spots on my face. She suggested the possibility of a chemical peel. Patiently, I explained that it was vitiligo, a medical condition.

Despite my sincerity, she began making insensitive comments, insinuating that I should feel bad about my appearance and that I would look better physically if I were in just one color. I explained to her that I have lived with this condition for forty years, and I have come to love and accept myself just the way I am. I do not feel any shame or regret for having vitiligo. I also shared with her that I am a mother and grandmother with far more significant concerns than the white spots on my face. The woman continued to insist that I would be "prettier" without vitiligo; I explained that I accept myself as I am. I politely told her my name, shook her hand, and said goodbye.

## Hitting Rock Bottom

Throughout this book, I have shared my experiences related to vitiligo and essential aspects of my personal life, which have been instrumental in my growth. It is relevant to talk to you about this part of my history. Despite all the negative experiences I've had in love, I began to believe again in the possibility of finding a good man who would love me and not use me. Unfortunately, I went through the most painful experience that broke my heart. This episode brought me to my lowest point and led me to reflect on myself deeply.

I met a man who made me believe he loved me. While I was looking for genuine love, he lied to me for years, making me think that he loved me to the point of proposing to me and marrying me. I thought I had finally found the man I had been waiting for so long, someone who would love me just as I am, respect me, and be faithful. However, after we married and I brought him to my country to start our life together, 2 months later, I discovered one of the most painful truths of my life: it had all been a lie. The shock and disbelief were overwhelming. He was not sincere, honest, or faithful to me. I realized the man I loved and respected was not who I thought he was; he had betrayed me. I was devastated to discover the truth. In my desperation, I turned to God, asking Him to heal my heart and guide me to recovery.

This painful experience was a profound awakening. I came to understand that my past wounds and childhood rejections had been influencing my choice of partners. But I didn't let this realization bring me down. Instead, I used it as a steppingstone for personal growth. I discovered an inner child in need of healing and self-love, and I set out on a journey of self-realization and healing. With God's unwavering support, I embarked on a mission to heal my inner child, forgiving myself for allowing myself to be in relationships where I wasn't valued and was used.

Through this process, I learned the importance of caring for and protecting the child I had neglected for so long. I made a promise to my inner child that I would always value, care for, and never abandon her again. These painful experiences ultimately led me to a profound self-discovery: I must prioritize and love myself first.

Vitiligo has been my companion since I was 4 years old, and despite the challenges, I found beauty in my authenticity. Now, I understand that my worth goes beyond physical appearance, and I deserve love and respect regardless of differences. I no longer allow people to put me down and lower my self-esteem because I know I am worth it. I deserve respect and true love.

Thank God, I have surrounded myself with people who love and respect me unconditionally. Their support has been invaluable in my journey to self-acceptance. Through adversity, I discovered the strength to face life's challenges with determination and courage, both in my personal and professional development. Those hurtful and cruel comments have lost their power over me. I gained a lot of confidence and can now confidently say that I am beautiful just as I am. Vitiligo is part of my story, but it does not define me. I am grateful because I have grown and learned much about myself on this life journey.

## *Looking to the Future with Hope*

I look at my present and future with optimism. I love myself as I am and know I deserve reciprocal love and happiness. I am willing to fight for meaningful, respectful, and reciprocal relationships. My journey has taught me that true beauty is found in self-acceptance and the value we give ourselves. There will always be people who believe they are better than you and want to use you and treat you as if you were worthless, regardless of whether we have a physical condition or not. It is better to be alone than in bad company. I am grateful for every experience that has led me to this moment of self-discovery and self-love.

# Chapter Eight

## ! A New Chapter in My Life!

Life took an unexpected turn when I embarked on a new adventure in the United States, leaving behind Colombia. Despite the daunting language barriers and the discouraging comments, my unwavering determination propelled me to learn English and pursue my academic and artistic goals. Each challenge became a steppingstone, a testament to the fact that with focus and dedication, anything is possible.

# *Focusing on My Goals*

In Colombia, I focused on studying Computer Engineering. Then, I decided to start a new chapter in another country with my daughter. When I came to the United States, I didn't know English. My strategy for learning the language consisted of watching television in English and living in an environment where no one spoke Spanish. This accelerated my language learning, as I was forced to speak English in any situation. Despite not knowing much about the language, I decided to study and pursue a career as an esthetician here in the United States.

Despite comments from people who said they couldn't graduate due to the language barrier; I persevered in my studies. I faced difficulties, especially in language, but I found the strength to graduate successfully, and I thank God for that. Whenever people told me I couldn't study yet because I didn't know English, it gave me the strength to move forward with my goals and show that I was capable.

In addition, I decided to pursue a degree in Fine Arts at the university. Each class and academic milestone marked progress toward my goal, reinforcing my determination to move forward.

After seven years of study—juggling a full-time job, raising my daughter as a single mother, and taking part in art exhibitions—I graduated in a degree in Fine Arts. Despite the challenges of single motherhood and full-time work, I stayed dedicated to my art, showing my work in galleries and refining my craft. This journey taught me that, with focus and dedication, I could achieve any goal I set. Throughout my career, God has opened doors for me, allowing me to display my art in galleries across the United States. My dream is to share my work in as many countries as possible. Art has become essential to my life, bringing me joy and a powerful way to express my emotions. Each brushstroke is an emotional release, giving me a unique way to share my feelings on canvas. This deep connection to art is an integral part of my journey.

## Encounter with God

From an early age, I began attending church, where I had a significant spiritual encounter with God that allowed me to be reborn. God made me feel that I am a valuable woman and that he loves me. Seeking God, I experienced love and acceptance in their purest form.

Every day, I find the strength to face the trials that life presents, supported by my faith in God, who is always by my side, providing comfort, guiding me, and reminding me of my worth and that I am her valuable daughter. Over the years, I cultivated greater strength and determination facing each challenge with courage and perseverance. This journey is a testament that I can overcome any obstacle with God. I am grateful for all the circumstances that I went through as a single mother. They pushed me to be better every day and to fight for my dreams and goals. But above all, I am grateful to God for always being with me in every moment, guiding me in every step I take, and giving me hope in the face of challenges. At this stage of my life, it is not the end but the beginning of new opportunities that are coming.

With every step I took on this path, I realized that the most significant barriers were not external but within my mind. The language, financial hardships, and responsibilities of single parenthood were not difficulties but steppingstones that propelled me forward. Instead of constraining me, they spurred me to find solutions and place more trust in the divine, who was my constant companion.

Looking back, I understand that it was not just my determination that brought me to where I am today but also the unwavering faith that kept me steadfast through the most challenging times, reassuring me that I was not alone. This phase of my life is not a conclusion but a gateway to new opportunities waiting to be seized.

# Karina Cuestas

Karina Cuestas-2024

k

*"God is my hope, strength in difficult moments, and light in the darkness."*

# Chapter Nine

## "Strength Through Adversity."

Life's trials, rather than weakening us, guide us through the ever-changing world. This chapter delves into the unexpected circumstances that reveal our inner strength. Drawing from my mother's example of facing challenges, each experience has been a steppingstone towards a stronger self.

# *"My Mother: An Example of Life."*

As life presents us with challenges and tests that shape our essence and find our course, I have discovered that each obstacle is an opportunity to cultivate an inner strength I never thought possible. The valuable lessons life has given me have made me a strong, brave, and hard-working woman like my mom.

My mother's example has been a profound influence on my life. Her courage and determination in the face of my father's abandonment made her an inspiration. She worked tirelessly to care for my siblings and me, ensuring we had a better life and meaningful opportunities. My admiration for my mom is profound. I saw her go to great lengths to ensure we had what we needed, even if it meant sacrificing her needs.

Her dedication to learning and belief in knowledge as a key to prosperity, her hard work, and her unwavering love are testaments to the power of education, perseverance, and compassion. These lessons I carry daily guide me through life's challenges and help me grow stronger with each obstacle I face.

My mother has always been a loving mother who prioritizes her children and instills in us strong values, such as respect for others. Her teachings gave me the determination and courage to face personal challenges.

## *Facing Challenges*

Like everyone, we all face difficulties in life. Each of us has struggles—some face many, while others face few—but as humans, we all meet unexpected circumstances that test us. Over the past forty-four years, I've been on a journey filled with unforeseen challenges. One of the most significant was raising my daughter as a single mother, working hard to secure a better future for her. Health problems, financial struggles, and matters of the heart were complex, but my faith in God kept me going. I want to share some of the challenges I've faced—those that have shaped my personal and spiritual growth.

One of the most significant challenges I faced over several years was my health. In 2016, I underwent a surgery that went wrong, leading to intense suffering and a recovery that lasted three and a half years. More recently, I battled COVID-19 and pneumonia, where I truly felt I was dying. After two hospitalizations, I relied on oxygen tanks for a year.

Recovery was slow, and even simple tasks like walking became nearly impossible due to my weakened condition. I also lost my job during this time, but I thanked God for providing me with everything I needed.

My recovery was a long and painful process. It took nearly a year before I could breathe without an oxygen tank. My lungs felt like they were full of heavy rocks, making it difficult to walk or even sit without losing breath, and I experienced a high heart race. The physical challenges were tough, but the mental toll was just as hard. I was depressed from being bedridden and unable to do basic tasks like cleaning my home, cooking, or driving. The isolation made it worse because I live alone. I prayed daily, asking God for patience and the strength to continue. I'm forever grateful for my family and friends who supported me during the most challenging moments of my life.

I began my recovery with short walks, just two minutes a day, gradually increasing as my strength returned. I had to go to physical therapy to help me regain strength in my lungs with time, but my faith in God was the most essential part of my recovery. Daily prayer, reading the scriptures, and looking for God gave me the strength to keep fighting, filling me with hope. Though I was on the brink of death, I surrendered my life to God, trusting in His will. I know He played a fundamental role in my healing and gave me the strength not to give up. Even when the trials are difficult, I knew God gave me the strength to keep going. Through my struggles, I discovered that every challenge is an opportunity for growth, and with faith and determination, we can overcome anything.

In facing these challenges, I also began to reflect on the importance of self-worth in relationships. I realized that choosing myself and prioritizing my well-being was essential to avoid being taken advantage of again. I find relief and peace in trusting that God has someone better in store for me. I believe in God's plan and want his guidance in every decision. I want to follow His will, knowing He loves me and wants the best for my life.

Looking back, I can see how every trial in my life, whether related to vitiligo, my health, relationships, or other challenging moments, was part of a grander plan. Each challenge was an opportunity for me to learn, a test of my faith, and help me for my personal growth. These experiences taught me to trust God completely, knowing He always guides me towards what's best. With these experiences, I now move forward with hope, understanding that God's plan for my life is far more significant than anything I could have imagined. The next chapter of my life is faith, courage, and new beginnings.

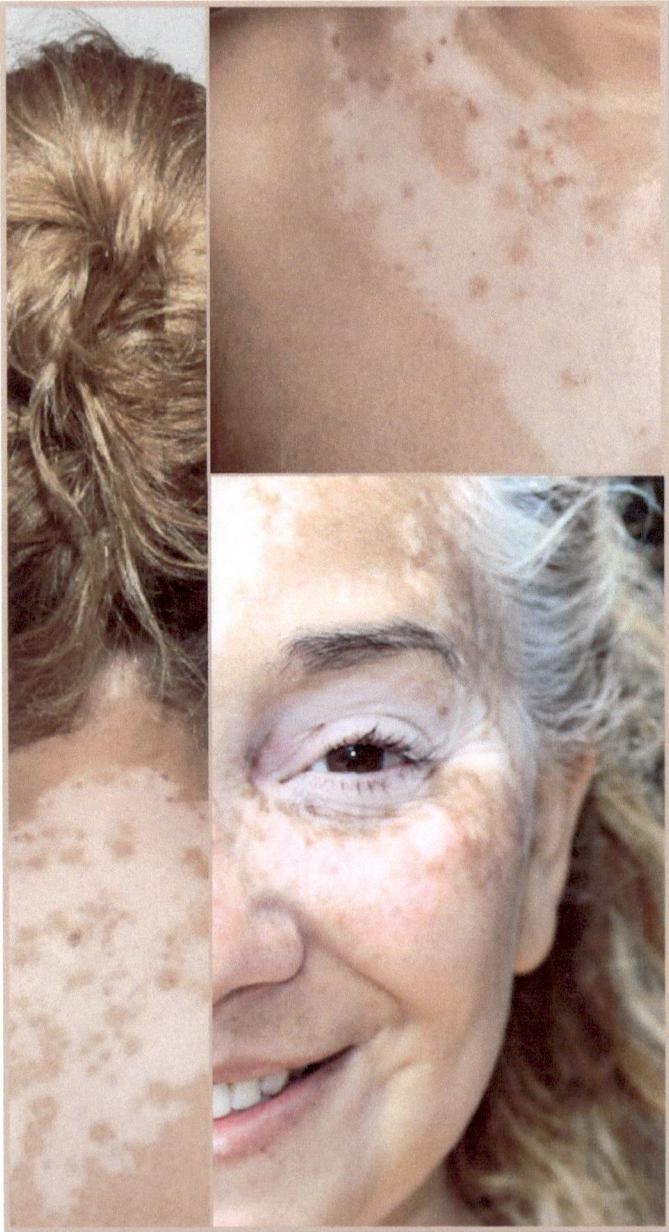

# Chapter Ten

## "Reflections of Strength: Embracing My Authenticity."

In this last chapter, we will explain the impact of vitiligo on those suffering from this disease. In a world increasingly open to diversity, we will explore how vitiligo has found a space of acceptance and empowerment. Join us in this chapter of understanding and self-love as we celebrate authenticity in those living with vitiligo.

# Self-Love

Vitiligo is a global reality, a condition that unites many individuals worldwide. This journey, though challenging, is also a source of valuable learning and understanding. Throughout my life, I have had the opportunity to meet people who suffer from this condition, and they have also experienced tough times due to the ridicule and stigma they face. I have a friend with vitiligo; most of his body has lost its pigmentation, making him feel sad and sometimes ashamed. My friend tends to dress in a way that covers his arms and legs so that other people do not find out about his condition since the vitiligo he suffers from is widespread throughout his body.

I recommended that he not be ashamed of his vitiligo and embrace and love himself as he is. I fully understand the challenges he faces because, in my case, I have already gone through a lot of psychological pain. After all, the vitiligo I have is in my face. I cannot cover my face. I sympathize with all the people in the same situation.

I have found that seeking support from friends and family and connecting with others with vitiligo can be incredibly helpful. I remember the first time I went out without makeup, exposing my vitiligo to the world. It was a liberating experience, and it made me realize that my worth is not defined by my skin color.

I want to convey a message of hope and strength and tell all people with this condition that vitiligo does not define us. On the contrary, the challenges we have overcome due to vitiligo have strengthened us, allowed us to empathize with others, and kept our humility. Our strength, our ability to overcome, is a source of inspiration for others. Vitiligo does not limit our worth; The loss of color in the skin does not condition our intelligence or hinder the goals we want to achieve.

I have learned to recognize my beauty and worth as a woman, friend, mother, grandmother, sister, partner, and colleague. Furthermore, I always remember that I am an appreciated daughter of God. You are a unique masterpiece, a valuable child of God. Your unique beauty, with or without vitiligo, is a testament to the diversity and richness of our world. Don't let other people damage your self-esteem. Your internal and external beauty and many talents make you a unique and valuable individual.

## New Era

In the digital age, vitiligo has gained global visibility, mainly due to the internet and social media increasing awareness and acceptance of this condition in society. People with vitiligo are now prominently featured in advertising campaigns, confidently highlighting their unique beauty. It is heartening to see that even children active on social media are growing up in a world where vitiligo is not a stigma. This growing awareness is a testament to the fact that, despite vitiligo, we are not less than anyone, and our beauty defies stereotypes.

My commitment is to bear vitiligo with dignity since it has been a part of me for forty years. I am not saying that I do not want to be cured; on the contrary, it would be good to find a cure. What I mean is that whether I am healed or not. My experience with vitiligo has shown me how strong I can be and how much I have learned from the adversity I have faced. It is a testament to my strength and ability to accept myself as I am, loving all sides of my being.

I want to emphasize that you are not alone in this journey of self-acceptance and love. You are understood and supported. We are a community and here for each other, embracing all sides of our being with love and acceptance. By raising our voices and supporting each other, we are committed to breaking down the barriers that society has placed on us. With more people with this skin condition, we build a path with hope, forming bonds of understanding. As I continue to paint the canvas of my life, each stroke shaped by lessons learned from the past, I find beauty in every experience, even the difficult ones. I deeply embrace the vibrant colors of self-love and am grateful for the blessing God has given me. Thank you for reading this book, and God continues to bless you all.

"Your individuality is a gift, and true beauty radiates from within. Never let anyone question your worth or accept mistreatment in exchange for acceptance. Embrace self-love, as it empowers you to love others fully. Stand tall, confident, and pursue your dreams boldly. Don't feel ashamed or less because your difference being is unique is a blessing. Remember, none of us are perfect, but you are deeply loved by God. You are His precious, unique, and beautiful child."

# *Biography*

I was born and raised in Ibagué, Tolima, Colombia. I have dedicated myself to Fine Arts, specializing in Abstract art. My canvas became a medium through which I could convey the depths of my emotions and create art. Today, at forty-four, I reflect on a life shaped by artistic passion and a unique personal experience living with vitiligo. Vitiligo not only left its mark on my skin but also contributed to my individual development. Over forty years, I have been on a journey of self-discovery, learning valuable lessons about loving myself. I discovered that a person's value transcends physical appearance. This discovery empowers us to embrace our uniqueness and find hope in our true essence. I have become a strong, brave, and determined woman, and I am to be surrounded by the love and appreciation of those around me. Through my story, I do not just share my experiences; I hope to ignite a spark in others and inspire them to discover our inner beauty, just as art has inspired me. My life is a testament to acceptance and strength, showing how these elements can help overcome adversity and reveal one's true essence.